BLADE
OF THE IMMORTAL

art and story
HIROAKI SAMURA

translation
Dana Lewis & Toren Smith

lettering and retouch
Tomoko Saito

Mirror of the Soul

DARK HORSE MANGA™

ABOUT THE TRANSLATION

The Swastika

The main character in *Blade of the Immortal*, Manji, has taken the "crux gammata" as both his name and his personal symbol. This symbol is also known as the *swastika*, a name derived from the Sanskrit *svastika* (meaning "welfare," from *su* — "well" + *asti* "he is"). As a symbol of prosperity and good fortune, the swastika was widely used throughout the ancient world (for example, appearing often on Mesopotamian coinage), including North and South America and has been used in Japan as a symbol of Buddhism since ancient times. To be precise, the symbol generally used by Japanese Buddhists is the *sauvastika*, which moves in a counterclockwise direction and is called the *manji* in Japanese. The arms of the *swastika*, which point in a clockwise direction, are generally considered a solar symbol. It was this version (the *hakenkreuz*) that was perverted by the Nazis. The *sauvastika* generally stands for night, and often for magical practices. It is important that readers understand that the swastika has ancient and honorable origins, and it is those that apply to this story, which takes place in the 18th century [ca. 1782–3]. *There is no anti-Semitic or pro-Nazi meaning behind the use of the symbol in this story. Those meanings did not exist until after 1910.*

The Artwork

The creator of *Blade of the Immortal* requested that we make an effort to avoid mirror-imaging his artwork. Normally, Westernized manga are first copied in a mirror-image in order to facilitate the left-to-right reading of the pages. However, Mr. Samura decided that he would rather see his pages reversed via the technique of cutting up the panels and re-pasting them in reverse order. While we feel that this often leads to problems in panel-to-panel continuity, we place primary importance on the wishes of the creator. Therefore, most of *Blade of the Immortal* has been produced using the "cut and paste" technique. There are, of course, some sequences where it was impossible to do this, and mirror-imaged panels or pages were used.

The Sound Effects & Dialogue

Since some of Mr. Samura's sound effects are integral parts of the illustrations, we decided to leave those in their original Japanese. We hope readers will view the unretouched sound effects as essential portions of Mr. Samura's extraordinary artwork. In addition, Mr. Samura's treatment of dialogue is quite different from that featured in typical samurai manga and is considered to be one of the features that has made *Blade* such a hit in Japan. Mr. Samura has mixed a variety of linguistic styles in this fantasy story, with some characters speaking in the mannered style of old Japan while others speak as if they were street-corner punks from a bad area of modern-day Tokyo. The anachronistic slang used by some of the characters in the English translation reflects the unusual mix of speech patterns from the original Japanese text.

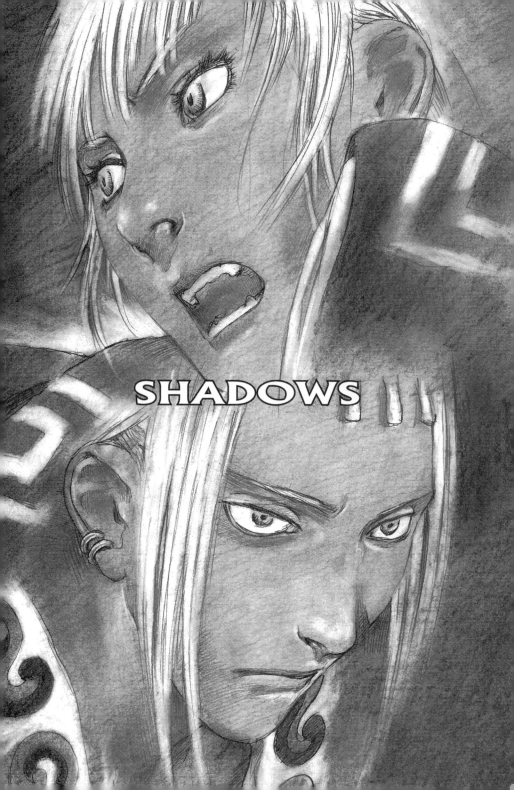

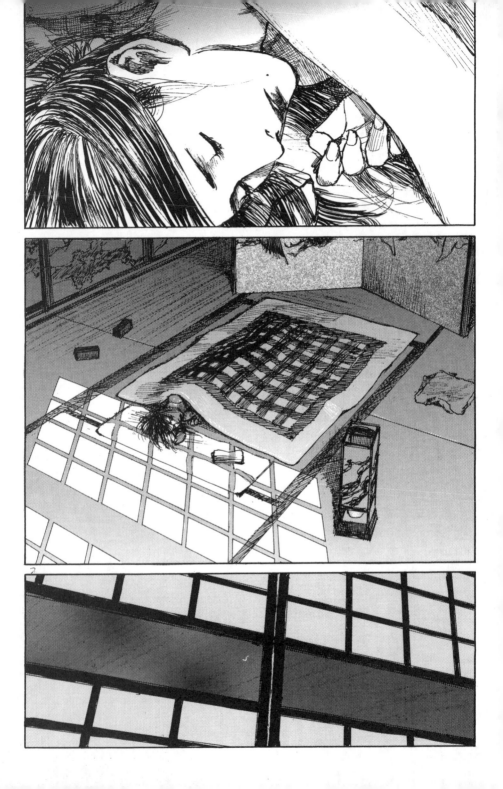

SO YOU'RE REALLY HEADED BACK...?

MM.

HOW IS KENSUI-*DONO*?

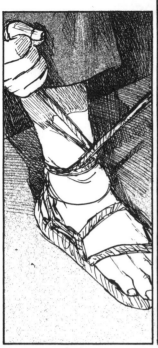

I HEARD HE COLLAPSED AT THE BANQUET. NOTHING SERIOUS, I HOPE...?

NO. PROBABLY JUST TOO MUCH *SAKE*.

THE MASTER DOESN'T LOOK IT, BUT HE TURNED SIXTY THIS YEAR.

STILL... IT'S JUST NOT *RIGHT*, ONLY ME HERE TO SEE YOU OFF.

SHALL I ROUSE THE YOUNG MISTRESS...?

NO... IT'S FINE.

THE CEREMONY AND THE BANQUET WERE PROBABLY HARD ON HER. I WANT TO LET HER REST.

NOW THAT THE YOUNG LADY'S YOUR WIFE...

...IT'S NONE OF MY BUSINESS, I KNOW. BUT... CAN I SAY ONE THING, ANOTSU-*SAN*...?

THE YOUNG LADY'S *REAL JOB* ISN'T TO BE YOUR WIFE.

IT'S TO BEAR AND RAISE YOUR *CHILDREN*.

SHE'S STILL A *SAMURAI* WOMAN. AT THE CORE, SHE'S A LOT STRONGER THAN YOU THINK.

IT'S NOT FAIR TO TREAT HER AS IF SHE'S... DAMAGED GOODS. IN MY OPINION, IT WILL ONLY MAKE THINGS WORSE.

AH...?

MASTER! HOW ARE YOU FEELING?

YOU JUST MISSED HIM... HE ONLY LEFT A MINUTE AGO.

IF I RUN, I CAN STILL CATCH UP. I'LL GO AND --

NO! KOZUE...

GET EVERY-ONE...

GET EVERYONE UP AND INTO THE *DŌJŌ*.

EVERY-ONE, UNDER-STAND?!

WHOO

IT'S...

KAGA...!

......?

K...
KAGA...?

......

.....!

koff

koff
shkk

......

nngh...

IT *WAS*
MOUNT
HAKUSAN!

SO...

SO, THIS
MOUN-
TAIN...

THANK GOD...

......
......

THANK G-
......

IN OTHER WORDS... I JUST USED MY LAST BIT OF STRENGTH TO CLIMB *OVER* MOUNT HAKUSAN, THE ONE ROUTE *EVERYONE* WHO GOES TO KAGA *AVOIDS.*

NO. IT'S OKAY.

JUST FORGET IT. IT'S *OKAY.*

ONCE I'M OFF THIS MOUN-TAIN...

I'M ALMOST *THERE...!*

WHEN I THINK THAT *MAN* IS OUT THERE, *SOMEWHERE* IN THIS LAND...!

WHEN I THINK *THAT*...

HEH HEH HEH...!

DAMN YOU, ANOTSU KAGEHISA! *WASH* YOUR NECK...

...AND *WAIT* FOR MY *BLADE!*

BUT DADDY...

THAT'S ONE OF THE OLDEST TRICKS IN THE BOOK. *IGNORE* HER!

NO... NO TRICK... ......

P- PLEASE... SOMEONE...

F... FOOD...

AH...?
YOU?!

YOU'RE SO *FILTHY* I COULDN'T TELL. ARE YOU *REALLY* ASANO TAKAYOSHI'S *DAUGHTER*?!

SNFF SNF?

THAT'S RIGHT!

I *AM* HER!!

WHAT ARE YOU DOING HERE?

"WHAT AM I"...?! ARE YOU *KID-DING*?!

YOU! I'M...

I'M LOOKING FOR... ......

....

>smf<

>hlkk<

......
......

WH- WHAT ARE YOU *CRYING* FOR?!

STOP IT... *STOP IT!!*

HOW'D YOU LIKE TO *USE* ME IN THE *ITTŌ-RYŪ*?

WELL...?

I REFUSE.

IT SEEMS YOU HAVE YOUR ENERGY BACK, SO I'M LEAVING.

......
......

WAIT!

DAMN IT! JUST *HOLD* ON A SEC!!

LISTEN, YOU! I JUST SAID SOMETHING PRETTY DARN *RADICAL* AND *UNEXPECTED*, IF I DO SAY SO *MYSELF!*

AT *VERY* LEAST, ACT *SURPRISED* OR SOMETHING!

WHY? IT WAS TOTALLY PREDICTABLE.

YOU'VE LEARNED ENOUGH ABOUT ME THAT I ASSUMED...

THE NEXT TIME YOU SHOWED UP... YOU WOULDN'T BE RASH ENOUGH TO ATTACK DIRECTLY.

I ASSUMED YOU'D TRY SOME SORT OF TRICK.

FOR INSTANCE... PRETENDING TO SWITCH SIDES.

......! ......!

H-HEY! WAIT A--

JUST TYPICAL *WOMAN'S* THINKING. NO SURPRISE AT ALL.

STILL, IT WAS WISE OF YOU TO LEAVE YOUR SWORD BEHIND.

I'M NOT *LYING!* IF YOU WANT *PROOF...*

I LEFT *MA-* I MEAN, I LEFT MY *BODY-GUARD* IN EDO!

YOU CROSSED THE *MOUNT-AINS*? A SINGLE WOMAN, *ALONE*?

Y... YES.

I'D LIKE TO PRAISE YOUR COURAGE, BUT...

YOU *FOOL!* YOU WERE COMPLETELY OUT OF YOUR *DEPTH!* NO WONDER YOU ENDED UP BROKE AND STARVING!

YOU SAY YOU WANT TO *JOIN* THE *ITTŌ-RYŪ.*

THEN LET ME TELL YOU MORE *ABOUT* US.

THE *ITTŌ-RYŪ* IS A SWORD SCHOOL... AND *NOT* A SWORD SCHOOL. A *TRADITION*... AND *NOT* A TRADITION.

WE OFFER NO *MEMBER-SHIPS*, NO SECRET *TECHNIQUE.*

IT'S UP TO EACH FIGHTER IF HE WANTS TO BUY IN, OR *NOT.* QUALIFICATIONS...? ONLY *ONE*-- THE *SWORD!*

HUH...?

······ GUESS NOT, HUH.

UM... ARE THEY WITH *YOU*...?

YOU THREATEN ME KNOWING WHO I AM?

I ASK *ONCE*, FOR YOUR OWN *GOOD*.

......

......

......

ANOTSU KAGEHISA... LEADER OF THE *ITTŌ-RYŪ*... WE TAKE YOUR *LIFE!*

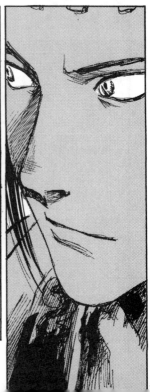

ASSAS-SINS...?!

AH-!!

DON'T MOVE! CONTROL YOURSELF!

SHOWING UP HERE WHEN YOU DID...

BAD LUCK FOLLOWS YOU, WOMAN.

BUT I'LL SAY IT AGAIN--IT'S A BLESSING IN DISGUISE YOU CAME UNARMED.

WHETHER YOU'D DRAWN YOUR SWORD *AGAINST* THESE MEN TO PROVE YOUR WORDS...

...OR *JOINED* WITH THEM TO TRY AND KILL ME, YOU WOULD HAVE *DIED* HERE TODAY.

BUT INSTEAD YOU SHALL LIVE... AND *LEARN*.

GO CURL UP IN THE ROOTS OF A TREE, AND *WATCH*.

AND SO... *FEEL* THE WEIGHT OF MY BLADE! *SCATTER* LIKE LEAVES IN THE WIND!

WH- WHAT SHOULD I *DO*...?

....?!

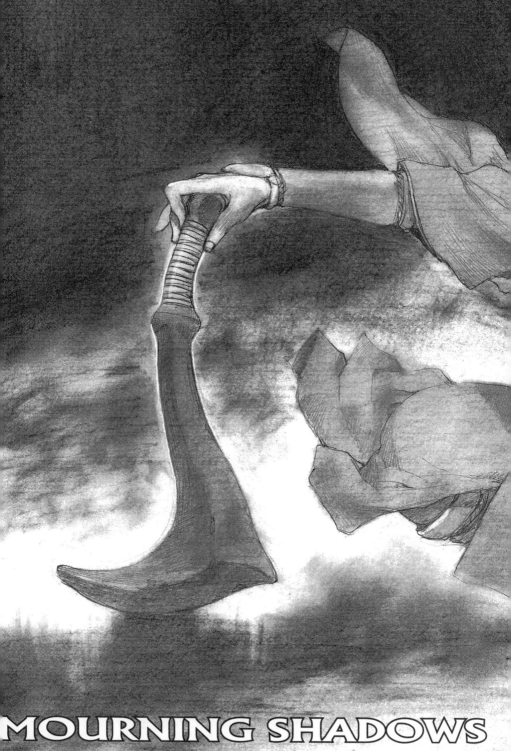

MOURNING SHADOWS

?!? EH--

THOSE MEN WHO KILLED MY FATHER, ASANO TAKAYOSHI, TWO YEARS AGO... AND CRUSHED OUR *DŌJŌ.* LESS THAN TWENTY OF THEM...

...GIVING ALL WHO STOOD IN THEIR WAY THE SAME, SINGLE CHOICE-- *"SUBMIT* OR *DIE."*

THE *ITTŌ-RYŪ.*

JUST TWO YEARS, AND NOW THEIR FOLLOWERS NUMBER MORE THAN A THOUSAND IN EDO *ALONE.*

VAST, YET ISOLATED. "THE SWORD SCHOOL WITHOUT A STYLE." "THE WILD BERSERKERS."

AND BEFORE MY EYES, THE FOUNDATION AND THE PINNACLE...

....ANOTSU KAGEHISA.

I SAY THIS TO YOU, JUST IN CASE.

IF YOU FLEE, I WON'T PURSUE.

.... SHIT...

GET INSIDE... THAT BLOODY HEAVY AXE...

IF I CAN GET IN-SIDE--

--I CAN *TAKE* HIM!

.... ! UUG!

NNG...
......

......
......
......

......
......
RRGHH!

......
IT'S OVER.

≳hnff≲

......
UM...

Y...
YEAH.

!!

......!

WHAT
TH-?

TWAP

AH?!

W--

WAIT! COME BACK! WHAT...

HEY!! THIS ISN'T FUNNY!

····· EEW.

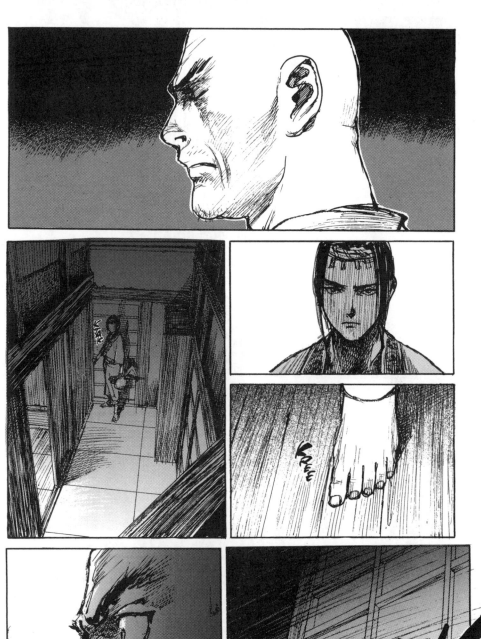

PATH OF SHADOWS

KENSUI-
DONO!

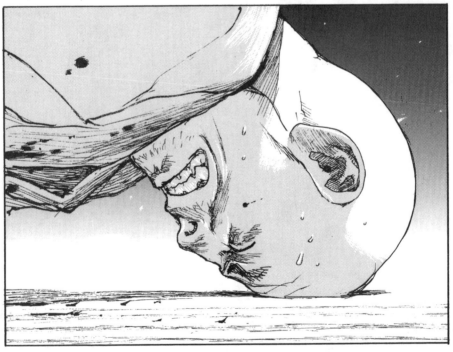

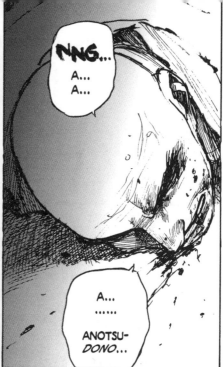

NNG...

A...
A...

A...
......

ANOTSU-
DONO...

SO...

MY
STUDENTS....

YOU
DEFEATED...
THEM
ALL...?

YES...

I SEE...
......

N-NO...
IT'S
BETTER
THIS...
WAY...

I AM THE **LEADER** OF THE *ITTŌ-RYŪ.* I'M USED TO HAVING SWORDS DRAWN AGAINST ME ON THE ROAD.

KENSUI-DONO...

MANY OF THE SWORDSMEN WHO'VE HAD THEIR *DŌJŌ* SEIZED BY THE *ITTŌ-RYŪ* REFUSE TO JOIN US.

MANY OF THOSE HAVE GONE TO GROUND IN THE COUNTRYSIDE TO FIGHT US.

BUT THERE IS NO REASON FOR **YOU** TO TAKE MY LIFE.

IF I DON'T GET A CONVINCING EXPLANATION, I WON'T PUT YOU OUT OF YOUR PAIN.

ANOTSU-
DONO...
YESTERDAY,
I...

DURING
THE
WEDDING...
YOU SAW
ME LEAVE
MY
SEAT?

YES.
I
REMEM-
BER.

AT...
AT
THAT
TIME...

AN
EMISSARY...
TOLD
ME...

"C...
CUT
YOUR TIES
WITH THE
*ITTŌ-
RYŪ*...

"...AND
TAKE
THEIR
LEADER'S...
LIFE."

AN
EMISSARY...
FROM
WHO?

.... TH- THE *BAKUFU*...

......! FROM THE *BAKUFU* ?!

GHKK

:koff:
:koff:

GOKK! GKK! KOKK!

KENSUI-
DONO...!

N-
NO...
DON'T
WORRY.

I
WON'T
DIE...
UNTIL I'M
DONE.

ANOTSU-
DONO...
PATHETIC IT
MAY SOUND,
BUT...

I HAVE
BUT ONE...
WEAKNESS.
STRIKE AT IT,
AND I AM
POWERLESS
TO RESIST.

THAT
WEAKNESS
IS--

NO.
I CAN
GUESS.

ONLY
ONE
THING
COULD
TIP THE
SCALE...

...FOR
ONE WHO
TREASURES
HIS
PROMISES
AS MUCH
AS YOU.

HISOKA-DONO'S *LIFE*.

....

Y-YES...

I WON'T TELL YOU ITS NAME. BUT IF SHE DOESN'T GET A *SPECIAL MEDI-CINE*...

WHAT *HERBS*--

N-NOT HERBS. NOT *CHINESE*. IT'S WESTERN... *FORBID-DEN!*

I HAD PLANNED... TO TELL YOU LATER.

BUT HER ILLNESS... IT'S FAR WORSE THAN YOU EVEN *SUSPECT*.

...IN TIME SHE BEGINS TO COUGH UP BLOOD. THEN, IN LESS THAN THREE DAYS, HER BREATH WOULD STOP *FOREVER*.

IT'S A HARSH DRUG...AND IN T-TIME IT WILL *BLIND HER*. BUT... HER LIFE C-COMES FIRST...

AND IT'S HER... ONLY HOPE....

"BEFORE... MY OLD MASTER FOUNDED THE *SHINGYŌTŌ-RYŪ*... HE WAS SWORD *SHIHAN* TO THE L-LORD OF MAEDA *HAN*.

"THAT BOND LET US... GET HER DRUGS... DESPITE THE BAN. INDEED, THE DAY Y-YOU ARRRIVED AT OUR *DŌJŌ*... I HAD GONE TO **COLLECT THEM**."

BUT... BUT BEFORE AN ORDER OF THE *BAKUFU*, SUCH BONDS ARE... AS NOTHING. THE EMISSARY TOLD ME...

"KEEP BUYING YOUR DRUGS, OR BE REFUSED THEM HENCEFORTH. ALL HANGS ON YOUR ANSWER!"

....
....

LAUGH AT ME... IF YOU WISH.

I NO LONGER UNDERSTAND... *ANYTHING*.

FOR TWENTY YEARS...

THAT CHILD'S HAPPINESS...

THAT'S ALL...

...*ALL* I THOUGHT OF... ANOTSU-DONO.

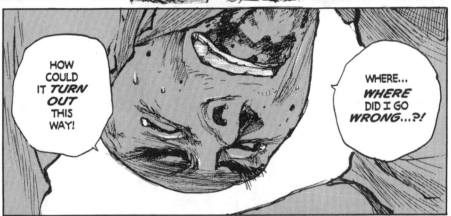

HOW COULD IT *TURN OUT* THIS WAY!

WHERE... *WHERE* DID I GO *WRONG...?!*

I UNDERSTAND... *NOTHING...*

THE ONLY THING I KNOW IS....

I HEARD MY... MASTER'S DYING WISH...

...AND *FAILED HIM.*

:koff!:

:koff!:

KENSUI-
DONO...!

A...
ANOTSU-
DONO...

I...
I AM
FINISHED.
I HAVE...
NO MORE
TO SAY.

I DON'T
ASK
FORGIVE-
NESS...
I HAVE NO
RIGHT.

ONLY,
PITY
THIS
FOOLISH
HEART...

THIS
SHAMEFUL
CHOICE...
I WAS
FORCED TO
MAKE...

AND IF
YOU
UNDER-
STAND,
PLEASE...
BE MY
SECOND.

KENSUI-*DONO*...

......
......
......

NO MATTER *HOW* MUCH YOU CARED FOR HER...

...YOU WERE A *FOOL* TO BETRAY YOUR OWN HONOR.

A WARRIOR CANNOT SERVE *TWO MASTERS.* IT'S MAKING THAT *CHOICE* THAT MEASURES OUR WORTH. IF THE TRUE PATRIOTS OF THIS LAND HEARD YOU WERE A PRISONER OF YOUR *FEELINGS*...

...THEY WOULD BE *STAG-GERED.*

......
......
......

AND YET...

WHAT I SEE IN YOU NOW...

...IS WHAT I SAW IN *MYSELF,* BUT FOUR DAYS PAST.

KENSUI-
DONO...!

I WILL
BE
YOUR
SECOND.

A...
A
WOMAN...?

LET ME EX--

NO. NO...

I HEARD... MOST OF IT.

LISTEN... IT'S A RULE OF THE *DŌJŌ*. AFTER AFTERNOON PRACTICE AND BEFORE THE EVENING BATH...

...KOZUE ALWAYS REPORTS TO KENSUI ON THE DAY'S PROGRESS.

SO... SOON ENOUGH...

...THIS WILL BE DISCOVERED.

AND BEFORE IT IS...

...IT WOULD BE WISE FOR YOU TO BE GONE.

IF YOU USE THE FRONT GATE, THEY'LL TRACK YOU EASILY.

LEAVE FROM THE BACK AND FOLLOW THE RIDGELINE OF THE MOUNTAIN.

...... MY THANKS.

IF... YOU HEARD...

WHY HELP ME *ESCAPE*?

KENSUI-*DONO'S* FEARS FOR YOU.

IF I FLEE...

...THEY *ALL* COME TO PASS.

KAGE-HISA!

I AM A *SAMURAI*, AND YOUR *WIFE!*

WHAT WIFE OF HONOR WOULD NOT SURRENDER *EVERYTHING* FOR HER HUSBAND?

......

F...
FAREWELL.

??
EH?

GET A GRIP, YOU IDIOT!

HE'S GONE...

FOLLOW HIM!!

WHERE'S THE BACK GATE...

THAP

ULP!

WHATCHA
DOIN'
HERE?

UH...
WELL...
ACTUAL-
LY...

JUST
A SEC...

THIS
COMPOUND'S
BEEN AT *FULL
ALERT* SINCE
MORNIN'...!

IF YOU
AIN'T GOT A
DAMN GOOD
ANSWER,
YER IN *DEEP
SHIT*.

SO
WHATCHA
GOT TO
SAY,
HUH?!

WELL,
I...
UM...
LOOK!

WHDD

≒hff≒

AH...?!

YOU!
WHY...?

WHAT IN THE WORLD...

...ARE *YOU* DOING *HERE*?!

I *TOLD* YOU, I'M FOLLOW-ING--

THEY'RE AFTER ME. I'M *GOING!*

WAIT! G-GOING? *WHERE*?!

WHO'S AFTER YOU?!

STEP-
FATHER...
*THANK
YOU.*

THANK
YOU FOR
A FLEETING
MOMENT
OF...
HAPPINESS.

I WAITED SO LONG FOR THAT MAN TO APPEAR.

THE MAN WHO COULD LEAD ME... NO...

SO *VERY* LONG...

...LEAD *US* FROM THIS DESOLATE MOUNTAIN.

BUT YOU KNOW, FATHER? AT THE SAME TIME, I SOMEHOW KNEW, FROM... OH, I CAN'T REMEMBER WHEN...

...THAT IF HE EVER *DID* APPEAR, HE WOULD JUST BE ANOTHER DREAM.

WHY *SHOULD* HE COME, AFTER TWENTY YEARS...?

AND SO... ISN'T THAT *RIGHT?*

FOR TWENTY LONG, LONELY *YEARS*...

...YOU LIVED IN THESE REMOTE MOUNTAINS, JUST TO KEEP YOUR PROMISE TO MY GRANDFATHER.

AND LOOK AT WHAT BECAME OF YOU... YOU POOR, *FOOLISH* MAN.

IT'S *ALL* OF US. TRAPPED HERE BY OATH AND OBLIGA-TION...

BUT, NO... IT'S NOT JUST YOU.

......
......

TO TELL THE TRUTH...

I KNEW IT FROM THE *VERY* BEGINNING. THE ONE WAY...

...THE *SIMPLE* WAY, TO SET US FREE.

I SHOULD HAVE CHOSEN THIS PATH... LONG AGO.

SNAP *OUT* OF IT, YOU *IDIOT!*

NNG... ...?

SHIT... WHO DUMPED WATER ON ME?!

HEY, GUYS!

WELL? WHAT HAPPENED ...?

huff huff

BAD NEWS... THEY'RE ALL *DEAD.* AND HE PULLED OFF MIZUMORI'S HOOD.

HE KNOWS NOW, MAN! HE *KNOWS!*

SO MUCH FOR OUR COVER-UP PLANS, HUH?

HEH... HEH HEH HEH HEH. ......

IT'S NOT *FUNNY!*

SHUT UP!!

DAMN, KOZUE... SO WHADDA WE *DO?* WE--

HUH...? WHERE'D HE GO?

......
......
......

HUH...
H-*HIM!*

IRIYA...
......

IT'S B-
BECAUSE
OF
HIM!!

FROM
THE
D-*DAY*
HE
GOT
HERE!

EVERY-
THING
WUH-
WENT
TO
SHIT!

WHOK

HOW C-
COULD...
HOW COULD
THIS H-
HAPPEN...?

AUUGH!

YOU B-
BASTARD!
IF *YOU*
HADN'T
CUH-
COME...!

ANOTSU!

KAGE-HISA!

......
MNN...
...?

I... I DON'T TAKE CHARITY...

AH. I SEE.

WELL, THEY WERE GIVEN TO ME YESTERDAY MORNING.

I CAN'T BRING MYSELF TO EAT THEM RIGHT NOW.

BUT THEY'LL GO BAD SOON.

SO IF YOU DON'T WANT THEM EITHER, I'LL TOSS THEM.

HEY, YOU.

HELP ME WITH THE BANDAGE.

GIVE ME A *BREAK!*

WHY SHOULD I HELP--

......
......

ISN'T IT ABOUT TIME YOU TOLD ME?

ABOUT WHAT?

WHAT YOU WERE DOING AT THAT *DŌJŌ* LAST NIGHT.

......

THERE'S NO POINT IN TELLING YOU.

MAYBE YOU DON'T THINK SO, BUT I'VE GOT A *RIGHT* TO KNOW.

I'M *ITTŌ-RYŪ*, TOO.

"*ITTŌ-RYŪ*"...? *YOU*?

I JOINED *YESTER-DAY!*

IS YOUR *MEMORY* SHOT?

LISTEN, GIRL...

...IF YOU JUST WANT TO PRETEND YOU'RE ONE OF US TO KILL ME IN MY SLEEP...

...GIVE IT UP. *NOW.* I DON'T BLAME YOU, BUT...

...THERE'S NO WAY YOU'RE *EVER* GOING TO KILL ME.

BESIDES, EFFECTIVE YESTERDAY, I'VE CANCEL-LED OUR AGREEMENT WITH THE *BAKUFU.*

I'M A *FUGITIVE* NOW. STAY WITH ME, AND YOU'RE A TARGET, TOO.

THE FUTURE'S *GRIM.*

THERE... DONE.

AH. THANKS.

....

THEY'VE GOT PEOPLE AFTER US. WE CAN'T USE THE MAIN ROADS.

AND SOMETIMES THERE WON'T BE *ANY* ROADS.

I GATHER YOU CAME OVER MOUNT HAKUSAN WITHOUT RESTING.

GOOD. BUT IF YOU BURN OUT THIS TIME, I WON'T HELP YOU.

IS THAT ACCEPT-ABLE...?

.... YES.

NEVER THOUGHT I'D CLIMB HAKUSAN *AGAIN*.

MUST'VE WALKED... TEN *RI*...?

AND ALL I'VE HAD TO EAT SINCE MORNING...

...IS A MOUTHFUL OF THAT DRIED RICE I BOUGHT LAST WEEK.

GREAT...I FINALLY MAKE IT TO *KAGA*, JUST TO TURN AROUND AND HEAD BACK TO EDO... BROKE, STARVING, AND NOTHING GAINED.

AAAH... WHAT A MESS.

CAN WE *REALLY* MAKE IT TO EDO...? WELL... *HE'LL* BE FINE.

BUT *ME*... ......

IS HE ASLEEP...?

MM... LOOKS LIKE IT...

YES! HE'S *SLEEPING!*

HEH HEH HEH...!

HA HA HA HA! *YES!!*

I'VE *WAITED* FOR THIS CHANCE...!

THAT "GOLDEN WASPS" TRICK OF YOURS... IT HAS A SERIOUS DEFECT.

IT WILL ALMOST *NEVER* KILL SWIFTLY.

AND SO... IF YOUR OPPONENT IS ANY GOOD AT ALL...

...YOUR HEAD WILL BE FLYING FROM YOUR SHOULDERS BEFORE YOU CAN EVEN TURN TO FLEE.

IT HAS SOME MERIT...

...BUT *ONLY* IF YOU HAVE AN ACCOMPLISHED SWORDSMAN BACKING YOU UP.

IF YOU'RE A *KENSHI*, KNOW YOUR STRENGTHS *AND* YOUR WEAKNESSES!

.... TELL ME...

...WHY DO YOU WISH TO BE A *KENSHI*?

WHY... ?!

WHY *ELSE* ?!

TO KILL *YOU!*

DON'T ACT *STUPID!!*

SO YOU KILL ME. AND THEN WHAT?

THEN I'LL... REBUILD OUR *DŌJŌ...*

...AND, AND...

......

I SEE... ......

WHATEVER. IT DOESN'T REALLY MATTER.

GO TOO FAR...IN *ANYTHING...*

JUST DON'T OVERDO IT.

...AND IT WILL ECHO DOWN THE GENERATIONS.

SOMEDAY-- IF YOU SURVIVE-- YOU'LL MARRY, LEAVE CHILDREN.

NEVER GIVE THEM REASON TO FOLLOW IN YOUR FOOTSTEPS, SEEKING FOR RETRIBUTION.

EVEN IF YOU DON'T INTEND TO DO SO.

OUR PREDECESSORS CREATED THIS WORLD OF "HONOR" WE LIVE IN.

FOR FAME. FOR *DUTY*. TO PROTECT THEIR *SCHOOLS*.

BUT LEAVING BEHIND A CYCLE OF REVENGE FOR THEIR *DESCENDANTS* TO TAKE CARE OF...?!

IRRESPONSIBLE! INTOLERABLE!

DO YOU UNDERSTAND?

NO! I DON'T!

YOU MADE ME CHOOSE THIS PATH! YOU!

I'M NOT GOING TO LISTEN TO YOUR EXCUSES NOW!

......
......
......

WHY...?

WHY DID YOU HAVE TO KILL M...MY MOTHER AND FATHER?

IF IT WASN'T FOR...THAT, I MIGHT BE ABLE...

...TO UNDER-STAND YOU... JUST A BIT...

GIRL...
I DID
YOU...

...*GREAT
HARM.*

WH...
WHAT...?

WHAT
DID YOU
SAY?!

ANOTSU
KAGEHISA...

YOU
BASTARD...!

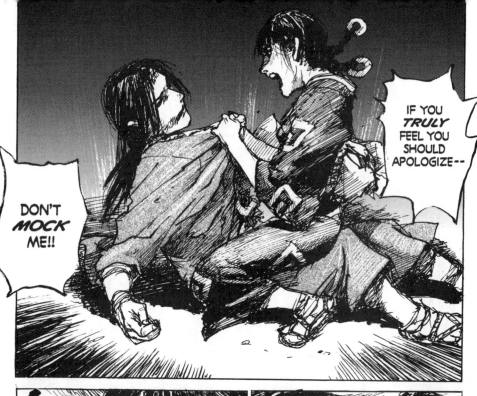

WE NEED TO CREST HAKUSAN AND REACH SHIRAKAWA BY TOMORROW NIGHT.

WE'LL LEAVE WHEN THE RAIN LIFTS.

IF YOU'VE GOTTEN EVERYTHING OUT OF YOUR SYSTEM... THEN SLEEP.

MIRROR OF THE SOUL
Part 1

......
......
......

WHAT THE HELL...?

SHIN-GYŌTŌ-RYŪ... THAT'S WHAT GIICHI SAID HE HEARD.

AND THIS IS THE PLACE, FOR SURE.

SO...WHAT THE HELL IS *THIS*? NO *RIN*... NO *ANOTSU*...

SHIT, NOBODY AT *ALL!*

HEY!

WHAT ARE *YOU* PUFFING AWAY FOR?! GET OFF YOUR BUTTS!

WE'RE HITTING THE ROAD!

AW, MAN... HAVE A *HEART*, BOSS. WE JUST *GOT* YOU HERE!

YOU LAZY *SLUGS!* YOU CHARGE ME AN ARM AND A LEG, AND YOU GOT THE NERVE TO *WHINE?!*

LET'S SEE... WE'LL HIT *KANAZAWA,* HOOF IT UP *KURIKARA* PASS AND THEN...

CAN'T WE TAKE A--

GOD... I FEEL SO *AWK-WARD*...

AND *FURIOUS...!*

ONLY... FURIOUS AT *WHAT?*

AT *MYSELF*, FOR FEELING AWKWARD AROUND *HIM?*

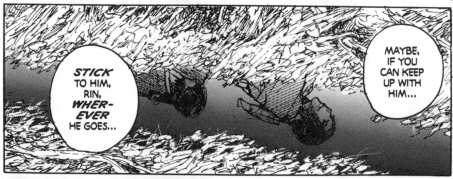

STICK TO HIM, RIN, *WHER-EVER* HE GOES...

MAYBE, IF YOU CAN KEEP UP WITH HIM...

...YOU'LL GET YOUR CHANCE TO TAKE HIM *OUT.*

HOLD *ON!*

WHAT? WORN OUT ALREADY?

VERY *FUNNY!*

LIKE *YOU* SHOULD TALK!

I JUST THOUGHT I'D MENTION SOME-THING.

I NOTICED *WAY* BACK, BEFORE WE STARTED, BUT...

...YOU'RE REALLY NOT LOOKING VERY WELL.

YOU THINK SO...?

YOU'RE WRONG.

OH, *AM* I...?

LIE TO ME, WILL YOU...? AS IF *YOU* DON'T KNOW IT, TOO...

MAYBE I *HIT* HIM TOO HARD...?

THAT'S HARD TO BELIEVE, BUT...

SHIRAKAWA VILLAGE

THEY'RE BURNING THE SUMMER FALLOW...

NEVER SAW THAT BEFORE...

WANT TO REST A MINUTE? WATCH A BIT...

SAY *YES!* DEAR *GOD,* SAY *YES!*

I CAN'T *TAKE* ANY-MORE...!

HERE.

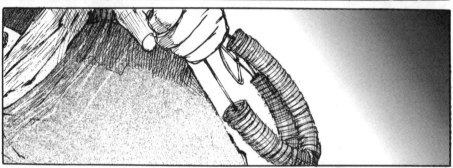

....!

I HAVE SOME... BUSINESS... IN TOWN.

YOU WON'T FIND ANY FANCY TEA HOUSES HERE...

...SO JUST BUY SOME DRIED SWEET POTATO FROM A FARMER.

YOU'RE... ≥hff≤ NOT JUST GETTING ME...

...OUT OF THE WAY SO YOU CAN TAKE OFF...?

HERE. TAKE THIS, TOO.

I DOUBT THEY'VE FOLLOWED US, BUT YOU MUST FEEL UNEASY WITHOUT A SWORD.

AH?! BUT... *WAI-*

NO. LATER.

B-BUT... ......?

NOK
NOK

YES...?
DO YOU WANT A *MINOGO* ...?

OR...
......
......

IT'S ANOTSU KAGEHISA.

I... HEARD YOU WERE HERE.

YOU, TOO...

DO I? NO...

JUST... TIRED FROM THE ROAD.

.... WELL.

WOULD YOU LIKE TO COME IN? REST A LITTLE?

OH... BEFORE I FORGET.

THERE'S SOMETHING I MEANT TO GIVE YOU, IF I EVER SAW YOU AGAIN.

......?

WHAT'S *THIS*?

MONEY. FOR WHEN YOU PAID OFF MY BROTHEL CONTRACT.

IT'S THE REMAINING BALANCE THAT I OWE YOU.

HOW DO YOU MAKE A LIVING?

THIS IS A TINY VALLEY, AS YOU CAN SEE.

IT'S *FREIGHT* THAT KEEPS THEM GOING.

THE VILLAGERS TILL A LITTLE LAND, THEY RAISE SOME SILKWORMS... BUT THAT'S NOT ENOUGH TO LIVE ON.

RUNNERS AND BEARERS-- *DOSHIMA* AND *BOKKA*, THEY CALL THEM-- CARRY CARGO BETWEEN TOYAMA AND GUJO.

I WEAVE A KIND OF PADDED RAIN CLOAK THEY USE, CALLED *MINOGO*.

AND THEY BUY THEM FROM ME. AND I SURVIVE.

AND... WHAT *ELSE*?

YOU COULDN'T SAVE ALL THIS...

...WITH HANDICRAFTS. STOP *LYING*. *TELL* ME THE TRUTH.

......
......
......

WHEN THE BEARERS AND FARMERS COME FOR THEIR... *MINOGO*...

I TAKE THEIR MONEY. AND THEN... I *SELL* MY *BODY*.

SATISFIED? DO YOU WANT *DETAILS*...?

HOW *COULD* YOU?!

KAGEHISA, *DON'T...!*

I AM *NOT...*

...AS *WEAK* OR *TRAGIC* A WOMAN AS YOU THINK.

I SIMPLY FOUND A WAY TO *SURVIVE* WITHOUT DEPENDING ON *ANYONE* ELSE.

I GAVE MYSELF TO IT... *GLADLY.*

IF I CAN LIVE QUIETLY IN THIS VILLAGE, WORKING DAY BY DAY TO FEED MYSELF....

...LEAVING NO MARK ON *ANYONE'S* LIFE...

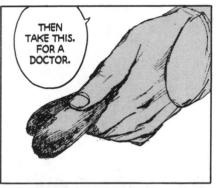

THEN TAKE THIS. FOR A DOCTOR.

......
......
......

I STILL WANT YOU BACK IN THE *ITTŌ-RYŪ.* THAT HASN'T CHANGED.

I'LL SAY NO MORE.

BUT... AT VERY LEAST, TAKE CARE OF YOUR HEALTH.

SAYONARA, MAKIE.

KAGE-
HISA-
SAMA!

I...
HOW...
UM...

H-HOW HAVE YOU BEEN? ANYTHING NEW?

NO, WAIT.

NOT MUCH.

ACTUALLY, I JUST TOOK A WIFE.

......
......
OH...

MAKIE...!

MIRROR OF THE SOUL
Part 2

TWAP

· · · · ·
· · · · ·
· · · · · !

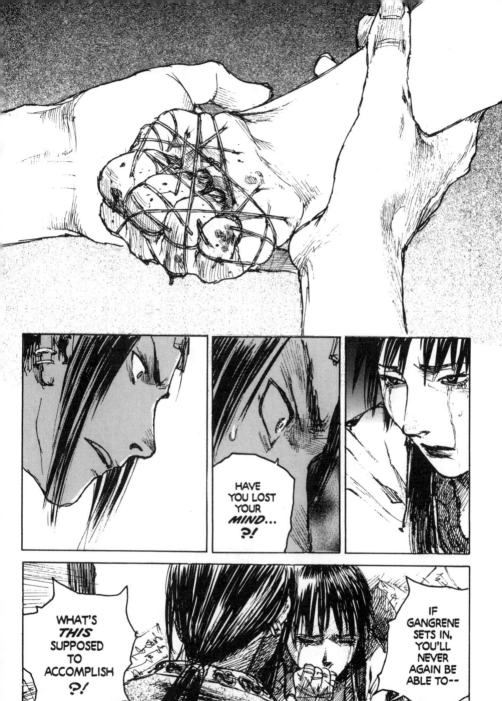

HAVE
YOU LOST
YOUR
MIND...
?!

WHAT'S
THIS
SUPPOSED
TO
ACCOMPLISH
?!

IF
GANGRENE
SETS IN,
YOU'LL
NEVER
AGAIN BE
ABLE TO--

KILLING, SPARING...

HATING, FORGIVING... *EVERYTHING!*

MAKIE...?
ARE YOU...
MAKIE?

EH...?
......
......

......
......
YES.

NNG...
......

AAH...
NO...

C-CAN
IT
BE...?

M...
MAKIE...?!

SHE WORE IT IN HER HAIR... THE DAY WE WERE MARRIED.

IT'S A FINE THING. MOTHER OF PEARL INLAY...

IT'S ALL BLACK WITH CAMELIA OIL, NOW...

......
......

I...I SOLD EVERYTHING ELSE TO GET MONEY, BUT...

...I COULD NEVER LET THAT GO.

IT WAS *FATE* WE LOST YOUR BROTHER.

I WANTED TO START A SCHOOL OF MY OWN... RUN MY *OWN* DŌJŌ, BUT... IT DIDN'T WORK OUT.

STOP IT.

HA HA HA...! *FUNNY*, ISN'T IT...?

AND AFTER YOU AND YOUR MOTHER WENT AWAY, I BROKE WITH THE *MUTENICHI-RYŪ.*

-koff-

AND NOW... SEE HOW I'VE FALLEN.

I WAS WANDERING THROUGH THIS TOWN WHEN CONSUMPTION STRUCK ME.

ALONE... ALONE ALL THESE YEARS. I KNOW I BROUGHT IT ON MYSELF... I KNOW IT WAS SELF-CENTERED OF ME, BUT... BUT...

THERE WASN'T A *DAY* GONE BY I DIDN'T DREAM YOU'D SOMEHOW HEAR ABOUT ME, AND COME HELP.

STOP IT!!

AHH... WHAT A GOOD CHILD. YOU ARE *SUCH* A GOOD CHILD!

......
......

koff
hck...!

FATHER
...?

THIS COMB... I'LL TAKE IT.

AND I PROMISE... I'LL GIVE IT TO MOTHER.

ALONG WITH YOUR WORDS.

YOU'VE GROWN UP SO *BEAUTI-FUL*... JUST LIKE *HER!*

HA HA... MAKIE!

OHH... ?!

OHH! YOU *WILL*?!

NEXT TIME YOU COME, I'LL BUY YOU A COMB JUST LIKE HERS!

SO GROW YOUR HAIR OUT, MAKIE!

MIRROR OF THE SOUL
Part 3

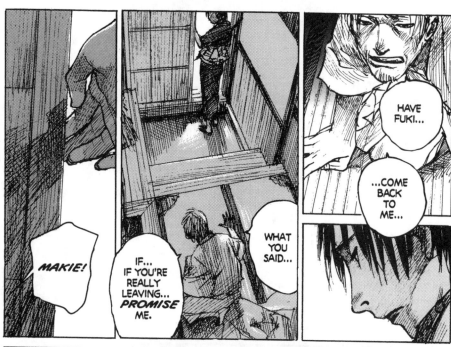

HAVE FUKI...

...COME BACK TO ME...

MAKIE!

IF... IF YOU'RE REALLY LEAVING... *PROMISE* ME.

WHAT YOU SAID...

YES.

ABSOLUTELY. I...

...I'LL BRING MOTHER. TO THE VILLAGE WHERE MY FATHER LIVES...

FATHER...

MY MOTHER... YOU KNOW WHAT...?

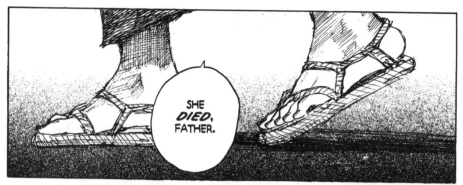

......
......
Анн...

≥snff≥
......
......

I...I'D PLANNED, AFTER KILLING HIM...

...TO KILL *MYSELF.* THEN AND THERE.

MY *MOTHER*, MY BROTHER, ALL THOSE OTHER INNOCENT PEOPLE...

NEVER *DESERVING* THE MISFORTUNE I BROUGHT THEM. THE MISFORTUNE MY *BLADES* BROUGHT THEM...

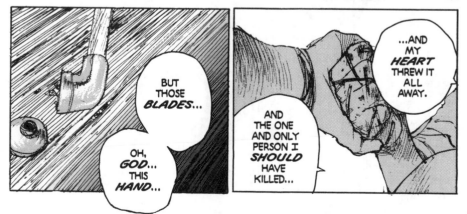

BUT THOSE *BLADES*...

OH, *GOD*... THIS *HAND*...

AND THE ONE AND ONLY PERSON I *SHOULD* HAVE KILLED...

...AND MY *HEART* THREW IT ALL AWAY.

SUCH A HOPELESS... *FOOL* OF A WOMAN. FADING AWAY LIKE THIS... NEVER SAVING ANYONE'S SOUL, PURGING ANYONE'S SINS...

...NEVER ACCOMPLISHING *ANYTHING* AT *ALL.* IT'S SO...

SO MISERABLE... SO... *TERRIFY-ING.*

......
......
......

……
……！

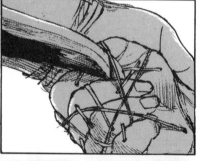

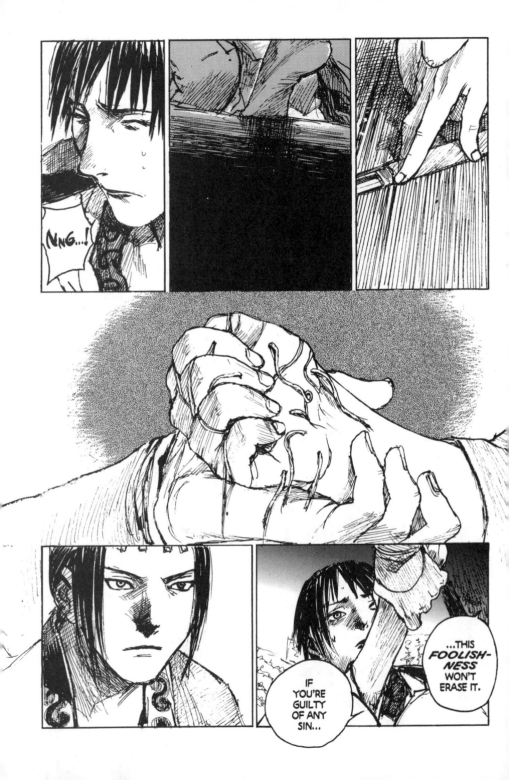

WE ARE *KENSHI!* ONLY THE *SWORD* CAN PAY FOR THE SINS OF THE *SWORD!*

ACCEPT IT! YOU'VE CROSSED THE LINE... STEPPED INTO THE *WHIRLPOOL.*

YOU CAN'T TURN YOUR BACK ON THE WORLD, OR PLAY THE CRIPPLE. YOU NO LONGER HAVE THAT *RIGHT!*

AND SHOULD YOU TRY... INDEED, YOU DO NOT DESERVE TO *LIVE!*

THIS *HAND*... NEARLY TEN DAYS SINCE YOU BOUND IT?

THE CORDS WILL HAVE HEALED TO YOUR *FLESH.*

BUT NO MATTER HOW MUCH YOU CRY OR SCREAM, I *WILL* NOT STAY MY HAND.

...RACKED WITH *UNSPEAK-ABLE* PAIN.

GRIP THESE SHOULDERS, AND *ENDURE.*

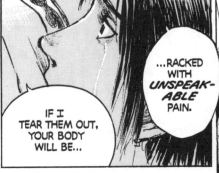

IF I TEAR THEM OUT, YOUR BODY WILL BE...

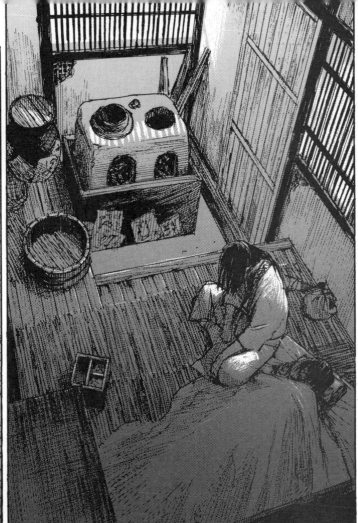

MY FIRST AND GREATEST MASTER...

I WILL NEVER FORGET THE DAY YOU SHOWED ME...

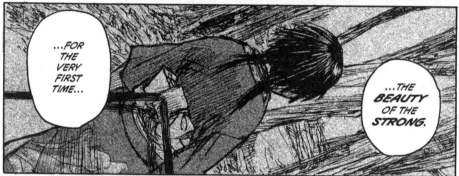

...FOR THE VERY FIRST TIME...

...THE *BEAUTY* OF THE *STRONG.*

...THAT GIFT ONLY *YOU* CAN WIELD.

I WILL NEVER, *NEVER* LET IT BE WASTED...

DID YOU GET SOME SWEET POTATOES...?

YEAH, AND I ATE THEM ALREADY!

I WOULDN'T *DREAM* OF ASKING *EXACTLY* WHAT *YOU'VE* BEEN UP TO, BUT...

...COULDN'T YOU ACT A *BIT* MORE LIKE A *WANTED MAN*?!

......
......
......

HERE. *YOUR* HALF.

WANT IT...?

...*RUN* ALL THE WAY TO EDO?!

DON'T TELL ME... THIS GUY... PLANS TO...

TH-THERE'S A HUT...

SHOULD WE...?

Y-YOU NEED... TO ASK?

NO. WE KEEP GOING... FAR AS... T-TAKA-YAMA...

?? HIS VOICE ...?!

......
......
......

LIGHT AND SHADOW

BUT... JUST OUT OF THE **BLUE?**

OH... I GUESS NOT...

BUT **HOW** ?!

WE ATE THE SAME **FOOD**... WHY JUST **YOU**?!

...I STILL SEE NO REASON...

IDIOT! YOU GET TETANUS FROM **WOUNDS**, NOT FOOD! BUT EVEN SO...

"TWO **DAYS** AGO...?!"

EH...? WHAT... **OH!**

NO, WAIT. THERE **IS** ONE...

BUT SUCH TRICKS ARE MEANINGLESS IN A *DUEL.*

THEY MUST JUST WANT TO GET ME, REGARDLESS OF *HOW.*

SO... WHAT WILL YOU *DO?* BACK TO *SHIRA-KAWA...?*

DON'T BE *STUPID!* WE *KEEP MOVING!*

IN *YOUR* CONDITION? WHO'S BEING *STUPID,* HERE?

I *HAVE* TO GET BACK AS SOON AS POSSIBLE.

THE EVENTS OF THESE LAST FEW DAYS... *ALARM* ME.

I THINK THEY WANT MORE THAN MY *LIFE.*

EVEN AS WE SIT, BACK IN EDO...

......

BACK IN EDO *WHAT?*

NONE OF YOUR BUSINESS, GIRL.

SO. HOW ABOUT IT?

ISN'T THIS THE PERFECT CHANCE...?

IF YOU WANT TO KILL SOMEONE YOU NORMALLY COULDN'T BEAT...

...WHAT BETTER TIME THAN WHEN HE'S *SICK*?

MAYBE SO. BUT... NOT NOW.

I UNDERSTAND NOW, I *REALLY* DO. DAYDREAMS WON'T CUT IT ANY MORE.

OR, ANYWAY...

HEH HEH

...NOT AS LONG AS YOU CAN *WALK.*

BUT! IF THAT TETANUS STUFF GETS WORSE...

...AND YOU CAN'T EVEN GET UP... THEN... WHO *KNOWS?*

I MEAN, *HONESTLY* SPEAKING? I THINK, IF I TRAINED AND TRAINED FOR TEN *YEARS* OR SO...

...THEN, PROBABLY... I *STILL* WOULDN'T STAND A CHANCE AGAINST YOU.

I'M IN NO RUSH. I'VE GOT *LOTS* OF TIME...

NO POSING ANY MORE... JUST *WAITING.* THAT'S ME.

HMM. AN *HONEST* GIRL.

AH...!
......
......

UM...
YOU *OKAY?*

HEH
HEH...

YEAH.
YEAH,
GUESS
IT
WOULD.

HEARING
YOU
WORRY
ABOUT ME...
MAKES ME...
REALLY
FEEL LIKE
SHIT.

SO LIKE,
I'M JUST
GUESSING,
BUT...

...DOES
IT *HURT*
TO
TALK?

THAT'S WHY I CAN TELL IT'S *LOCK-JAW.* AS THE DISEASE PROGRESSES, IT AFFECTS THE... MUSCLES OF THE JAW. EVENTUALLY... WON'T BE ABLE TO TALK AT ALL.

YOU NOTICED ...?

OH... *LOCK-JAW*?!

I'VE HEARD OF THAT.

BUT... I DON'T GET IT.

FOR SOMEONE RAISED IN A *SAMURAI* HOUSEHOLD, YOU SURE KNOW A LOT ABOUT IT. I MEAN, ISN'T IT A *FARMER'S* DISEASE...?

AS I TOLD YOU...

...IT IS A *WEAPON OF WAR.* AND I...HAVE STUDIED WAR ALL MY LIFE.

THE CORE PHILOSOPHY OF THE ITTŌ-*RYŪ* IS... "WHATEVER WORKS."

SO I... ....

AREN'T
THEY...
FROM
THE
DŌJŌ?!

YES...THE *TRUE* FACE OF OUR ATTACKERS.

WH... WHAT DO WE *DO?*

HIDE UNTIL THEY LEAVE?!

......
......

NO... H- *HOPE- LESS.*

FOR... VARIOUS REASONS...

...THEY HAVE NOWHERE TO GO HOME TO.

I'M SURE THEY'VE STAKED OUT EVERY ROUTE... THEY'LL CHASE ME ALL THE WAY TO EDO.

AND AS WEAKENED AS I AM NOW...CAN'T POSSIBLY EVADE THEM ALL.

SOMETIME, SOME- WHERE... I'LL *HAVE* TO FIGHT.

BUT... CAN YOU STILL *WIN*?

I... I DON'T KNOW.

SO IT MUST TO BE *HERE* AND *NOW*... WHILE I CAN STILL *MOVE!*

THESE AREN'T MEN I COULD TAKE IN A SINGLE BREATH...

...EVEN AT THE *BEST* OF TIMES.

AND NOW, IF I FACE THEM ONE BY ONE... I'LL RUN OUT OF ENERGY BEFORE THEY'RE ALL DOWN.

SHEESH... YOU'RE AWFULLY *CALM* ABOUT IT.

SO... THAT MEANS IT'S *HOPE- LESS*?

NO... THERE'S STILL ONE *POSSIBLE* PATH TO VICTORY.

REMEMBER... WHAT I SAID IN THE *CAVE*?

...?!

YEAH... THEY FOUND HIS BLOOD ON ONE OF THEIR SWORDS.

YOU THINK WE *PASSED* 'EM?

NAW. NOT LIKELY.

JUST WASTED EFFORT. AND HE DOESN'T *WASTE* EFFORT, NOT *THAT* GUY.

....

HE AIN'T GONNA BE MOVIN' TOO FAST... NOT WITH *LOCKJAW.*

AND EVEN IF HE COULD, HE KNOWS WE'D BLOCK ALL THE PATHS TO EDO.

GEEZ... TEN DAYS AGO WE WERE JUST RUNNING AROUND ON *TATAMI,* SWINGING *BOKUTO* ALL DAY.

HOW'D WE END UP LIKE *THIS*?!

SEE?! I FRIGGIN' *TOLD* YOU GUYS!

"THAT DUDE FROM EDO IS BAD NEWS, MAN," I TOLD YA!

WILL YOU ASSHOLES JUST *SHUT UP*?!

OKAY ...?!

MAN!

NOW REMEMBER! WHEN YOU *SEE* THE BASTARD, *NO SHOWING OFF!*

MASS ATTACK! *TOGETHER!*

OKAY, OKAY...!

GEEZ...

THIS ISN'T A *DUEL*, IT'S A *FUNERAL!*

WE'VE *GOT* TO TAKE HIM, OUTCLASSED OR *NOT.*

HUH?

WHAT'S WITH THAT *BROAD* ...?

...??

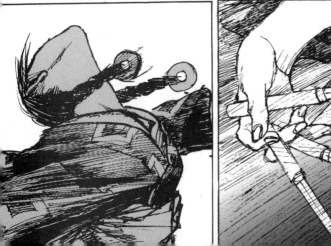

YOU LITTLE *BITCH!*

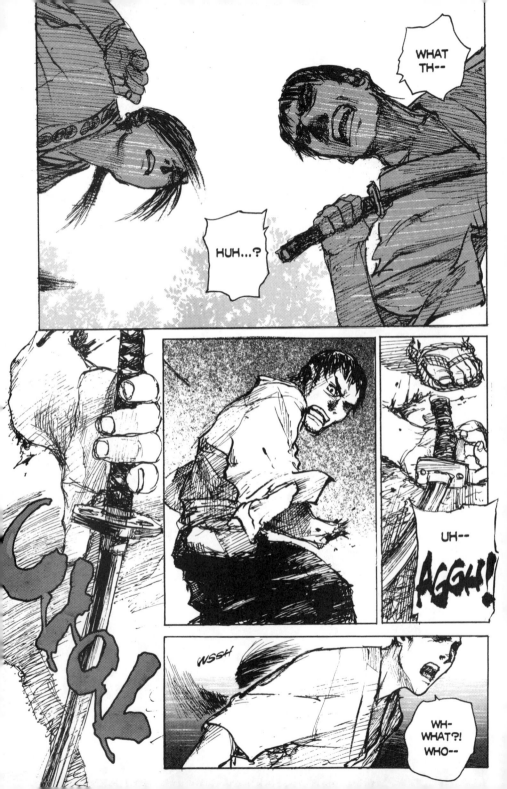

AAA!

...?

EH?

HE CIRCLED *AROUND!!*

BUT...
WAI--

SPANNGG!!

NNG!

AUGGH!

UH...
......

LET'S GO.

AAH.. NNG...

ANOTSU *KAGE-HISA!*

THIS ISN'T OVER, YOU *BASTARD!*

IF IT WASN'T FOR *YOU*... THE *MASTER* AND THE *MISTRESS*...

...THEY *NEVER* WOULD HAVE...

WE'LL **KILL YOU,** ANOTSU KAGEHISA **!!**

WE'LL FIND YOU! WE'LL **GET YOU!**

THAT RISKY STRATEGY... ......

I DIDN'T THINK YOU'D AGREE SO EASILY.

HMM. YOU SURPRISED ME.

EH?

AFTER ALL... IF I COULDN'T KILL THEM ALL, AND THEY GOT **ME**... WHY SHOULD **YOU** CARE?

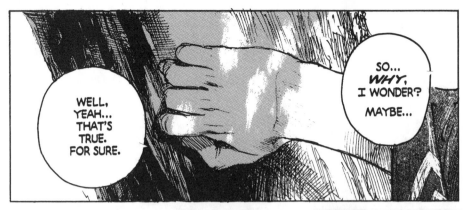

SO...
WHY,
I WONDER?
MAYBE...

WELL,
YEAH...
THAT'S
TRUE.
FOR SURE.

...'CAUSE
IT'D
*PISS
ME
OFF!*

YOU
GETTING
YOURSELF
KILLED WHEN
IT DIDN'T HAVE
ANYTHING
TO DO WITH
MY STUFF!

YOU
KNOW...
YOU'RE
SOME PIECE
OF WORK,
GIRL.

WHY,
THANK
YOU, SIR!
SO *VERY*
MUCH!

CROSSROADS

......

......!

OH, YEAH. MINE, TOO.

HERE. MY SWORD.

UH... UM... YES, SIR!

..... HRM!

A SPLENDID SIGHT...

...ABAYAMA-DONO!

HA HAHA! HERE, HABAKI-DONO... TAKE THIS.

FOR A TOAST!

MY THANKS.

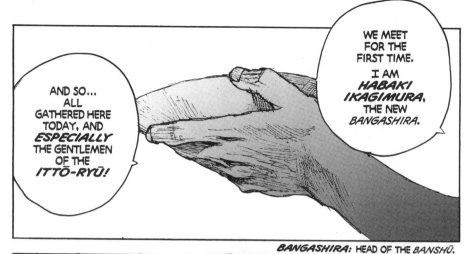

WE MEET FOR THE FIRST TIME. I AM *HABAKI IKAGIMURA,* THE NEW *BANGASHIRA.*

AND SO... ALL GATHERED HERE TODAY, AND *ESPECIALLY* THE GENTLEMEN OF THE *ITTŌ-RYŪ!*

BANGASHIRA: HEAD OF THE *BANSHŪ.*

WE OF THE *BANSHŪ* OFFER OUR PROFOUNDEST THANKS...

...FOR YOUR GRACIOUS AID IN THE ESTABLISHMENT OF OUR NEW *KŌKENJO.*

NOW, IF THIS WAS ONE OF OUR STIFF *BANSHŪ* AFFAIRS...

...I MIGHT *EXPOUND* UPON THE DECLINE OF THE *WARRIOR SPIRIT* THESE DECADES PAST.

BUT...

IT'S ABSURD TO DRONE ON WITH A *FULL CUP* IN MY HAND!

ESPECIALLY WHEN I SEE SOME *CHOPSTICKS* AT THE READY!

HA HA HA!

I DEEPLY REGRET THAT THE ITTŌ-*RYŪ'S* LEADER, ANOTSU KAGEHISA-*DONO,* COULD NOT JOIN US.

YET IF OUR HEARTFELT LITTLE FEAST PROVIDES...

...AN OPPORTUNITY TO STOKE THE FIRES AND FLESH OF YOU WILD WARRIORS, WHAT *MORE* COULD I ASK?

DIG IN!!

YOU!!

HEY, BIG *SPENDER!*

NICE SPREAD!

"BIG SPENDER"...? NOT I. BUT SERIOUSLY, ABAYAMA-DONO...

...IS THIS REALLY ACCEPTABLE?

I REFER, OF COURSE, TO THE ABSENCE OF ANOTSU-DONO.

DON'T GIVE HIM ANOTHER THOUGHT, HABAKI-*DONO*.

IT'S *HIS* FAULT FOR NOT BEING BACK WHEN HE'D BE.

YET... WE COULD HAVE RESCHEDUL-ED...

NO, NO.

WHY WASTE MORE OF YOUR BUDGET? KAGEHISA DOESN'T CARE ABOUT THINGS LIKE THIS.

I UNDER-STAND MANY HAVE DESIGNS ON ANOTSU-*DONO*'S LIFE.

PERHAPS THIS TRIP AS WELL...?

AND I HEAR YOU AND YOUR PEOPLE WENT TO CONSIDERABLE *PAINS* WHEN HE LEFT FOR KAGA?

YES, YES... ALL TRUE. HOWEVER...

YOU SEE, HABAKI-*DONO*... THE REASON WE CAN KICK BACK LIKE THIS AND *ENJOY*...

...IS BECAUSE WE KNOW OUR BOSS'S *SWORD ARM* DESERVES *ALL* THE TRUST WE PUT IN IT.

BUT GENERALLY... *YES*. UNLESS HE WAS SICK OR INJURED, OF COURSE.

SO, YOU FEEL THERE'S *NOTHING* THE YOUNG GENIUS OF THE ITTŌ-*RYŪ* CAN'T HANDLE?

NOTHING AT ALL...?

HA HA HA!

"*GENIUS*"...? TOO MUCH!

;ahh;

DAMN GOOD *SAKE!*

I KNOW WHAT YOU MEAN. I'M ALWAYS GETTING ON OUR YOUNG'UNS CASE ABOUT THAT.

BUT I WAS PRETTY FULL OF MYSELF, TOO, WHEN I WAS YOUR AGE.

FORTY-EIGHT.

SO *YOUNG!* I'M SIXTY-FIVE.

BY THE WAY... HOW OLD *ARE* YOU, HABAKI-*DONO?*

HRMM... YES...I SEE. PERHAPS A MEASURE OF COMPLACENCY ISN'T BAD WHEN YOU'RE *YOUNG.* NO, *CERTAINLY* NOT!

YET TO STRUT ABOUT IN ARROGANCE WHEN YOUR SKILLS CAN'T BEGIN TO MATCH THOSE OF THE WARRIORS OF OLD APPEARS MERELY... *COMICAL.*

MUSH-ROOM AND FERN TIP *NUTA.*

MM... *DELI-CIOUS!* WHAT IS IT?

HA HA HA!

ANYWAY, THAT'S WHY--*HOH?* WHERE TO?

EXCUSE ME... THE BATH ROOM.

~whewww~

HUH...
SO MUCH
FOR THE
GREAT LEADER
OF THE
ITTO-*RYŪ*

CATCHES
A BUG,
AND HE'S
DOWN LIKE
THE REST
OF US.

COUPLE
DAYS AGO
HE COULD
STILL
FIGHT.

AND
NOW HE
CAN'T EVEN
WALK
WITHOUT
MY
HELP.

DARN
IT...
......

YOU'RE
NOT THE
ONLY
ONE WHO
NEEDS A
REST...

?

WHAT?
YOU
WANT
ME?

"WHY"...

"NOT"...

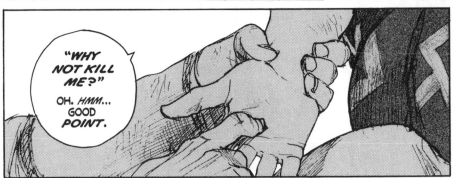

"WHY NOT KILL ME?"

OH. *HMM*... GOOD *POINT*.

HOW DO I *PUT* THIS...? MAYBE...

"I MISSED MY WINDOW OF OPPORTUNITY"...?

I MEAN, *KILLING* SOMEONE WHO CAN'T EVEN *STAND UP*...?

IT JUST SEEMS KIND OF *SLEAZY*, YOU KNOW?

......
......

......?

HERE.

YOU'VE DRAGGED THAT SICK BODY OF YOURS ALL THE WAY TO *SUWA*.

YOU'VE DONE *REALLY* WELL.

BUT IT'S *OVER*, RIGHT? YOU'VE REACHED THE *END*, RIGHT? YOU'LL NEVER RECOVER FROM THAT DISEASE UNLESS YOU GET SOME DECENT FOOD AND SHELTER.

BUT WE CAN'T EVEN USE A *FLOPHOUSE* OR THEY'LL TRACK US DOWN.

AND YOU'LL *STILL* HAVE TO FIGHT THEM, SOMEWHERE, *SOMEHOW*, BEFORE WE REACH EDO.

NOW, *THIS* STUFF...

...IT'S NOT MEDICINE.

IT'S *BUSU*.

BUSU: A POISON, EXTRACT OF MONKSHOOD

WILL YOU *WIN* THIS TIME? I DON'T *THINK* SO. YOU CAN'T EVEN SWING YOUR *AXE!*

FRIEND OR FOE, I THINK ANYONE WHO'S BEEN PUSHED THIS FAR...

...AT LEAST DESERVES THE *CHOICE.*

......

......

GSSSH

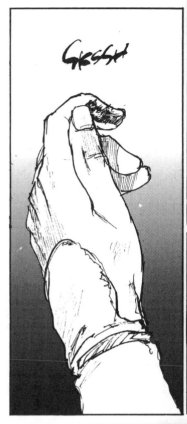

HEH... YOU'RE *HOPE- LESS...!*

SO *BE* IT! THEN I'LL WATCH OVER YOU... TO YOUR *END.*

TO BE CONTINUED...

GLOSSARY

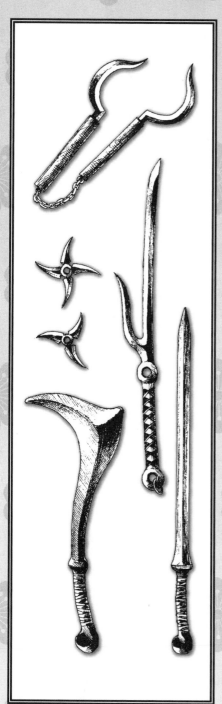

bakufu: a military arm of early Japanese government, concerned primarily with military and police matters. Also referred to as the "tent government," because soldiers lived in tents.

bangashira: head of the *banshū*

banshū: officers serving under the Shogun, usually assigned to Edo castle to defend the Shogun himself

bokuto: a sword made of wood

busu: a poison made by sun-drying the root of the *torikabuto* (Monkshood) plant

dōjō: a hall for martial arts training; here centers for swordsmanship

dono: a very polite honorific indicating much respect

han: a feudal domain

Ittō-ryū: the radical sword school of Anotsu Kagehisa

Kaga: a remote feudal domain on the Japan Sea coast southwest of Edo

kenshi: a swordsman (or swordswoman), not necessarily born into the samurai caste

kōkenjo: sword school established by the Shogunate

Mutenichi-ryū: the sword school led by Rin's father

nuta: a Japanese dish mixing fish or vegetables with miso, rice vinegar, sesame seeds, and other ingredients

ri: old Japanese unit of measurement equivalent to 2.44 miles

ryū: a sword school

shihan: a respected, official instructor

tatami: a thick, rice straw mat used as flooring in traditional Japanese households, still commonly found in at least one room of a residence even today

KOSUKE FUJISHIMA'S
Oh My Goddess!

The stories following the misadventures of Keiichi Morisato and the trio of lovely goddesses who live with him explode into a fantastic romantic comedy!

Volume 1
WRONG NUMBER
160-page B&W paperback
ISBN: 1-56971-669-2 $13.95

Volume 2
LEADER OF THE PACK
152-page B&W paperback
ISBN: 1-56971-764-8 $13.95

Volume 3
FINAL EXAM
152-page B&W paperback
ISBN: 1-56971-765-6 $13.95

Volume 4
LOVE POTION NO. 9
192-page B&W paperback
ISBN: 1-56971-252-2 $14.95

Volume 5
SYMPATHY FOR THE DEVIL
160-page B&W paperback
ISBN: 1-56971-329-4 $12.95

Volume 6
TERRIBLE MASTER URD
176-page B&W paperback
ISBN: 1-56971-369-3 $12.95

Volume 7
THE QUEEN OF VENGEANCE
152-page B&W paperback
ISBN: 1-56971-431-2 $13.95

Volume 8
MARA STRIKES BACK
176-page B&W paperback
ISBN: 1-56971-449-5 $14.95

Volume 9
NINJA MASTER
152-page B&W paperback
ISBN: 1-56971-474-6 $13.95

Volume 10
MISS KEIICHI
232-page B&W paperback
ISBN: 1-56971-522-X $16.95

Volume 11
THE DEVIL IN MISS URD
176-page B&W paperback
ISBN: 1-56971-540-8 $14.95

Volume 12
THE FOURTH GODDESS
280-page B&W paperback
ISBN: 1-56971-551-3 $18.95

Volume 13
CHILDHOOD'S END
216-page B&W paperback
ISBN: 1-56971-685-9 $15.95

Volume 14
QUEEN SAYOKO
240-page B&W paperback
ISBN: 1-56971-766-4 $16.95

Volume 15
HAND IN HAND
256-page B&W paperback
ISBN: 1-56971-921-7 $17.95

Volume 16
MYSTERY CHILD
272-page B&W paperback
ISBN: 1-56971-950-0 $17.95

Volume 17
TRAVELER
256-page B&W paperback
ISBN: 1-56971-986-1 $17.95

Volume 18
THE PHANTOM RACER
264-page B&W paperback
ISBN: 1-59307-217-1 $15.95

DON'T MISS THESE OTHER FANTASTIC TITLES FROM DARK HORSE MANGA AND STUDIO PROTEUS!

AKIRA
Katsuhiro Otomo
Book 1
364-page B&W / 1-56971-498-3 / $24.95

Book 2
304-page B&W / 1-56971-499-1 / $24.95

Book 3
288-page B&W / 1-56971-525-4 / $24.95

Book 4
400-page B&W / 1-56971-526-2 / $27.95

Book 5
416-page B&W / 1-56971-527-0 / $27.95

Book 6
440-page B&W / 1-56971-528-9 / $29.95

ASTRO BOY
Osamu Tezuka
Volume 1
224-page B&W / 1-56971-676-5 / $9.95

Volume 2
208-page B&W / 1-56971-677-3 / $9.95

Volume 3
208-page B&W / 1-56971-678-1 / $9.95

Volume 4
216-page B&W / 1-56971-679-X / $9.95

Volume 5
216-page B&W / -56971-680-3 / $9.95

Volume 6
232-page B&W / 1-56971-681-1 / $9.95

Volume 7
216-page B&W / 1-56971-790-7 / $9.95

Volume 8
200-page B&W / 1-56971-791-5 / $9.95

Volume 9
216-page B&W / 1-56971-792-3 / $9.95

Volume 10
216-page B&W / 1-56971-793-1 / $9.95

Volume 11
216-page B&W / 1-56971-812-1 / $9.95

Volume 12
224-page B&W / 1-56971-813-X / $9.95

Volume 13
224-page B&W / 1-56971-894-6 / $9.95

Volume 14
224-page B&W / 1-56971-895-4 / $9.95

Volume 15
232-page B&W / 1-56971-896-2 / $9.95

Volume 16
256-page B&W / 1-56971-897-0 / $9.95

Volume 17
216-page B&W / 1-56971-898-9/ $9.95

Volume 18
216-page B&W / 1-56971-899-7 /$9.95

Volume 19
216-page B&W / 1-56971-900-4 / $9.95

Volume 20
224-page B&W / 1-56971-901-2 / $9.95

Volume 21
232-page B&W / 1-56971-902-0 / $9.95

Volume 22
216-page B&W / 1-56971-903-9 / $9.95

Volume 23
192-page B&W / 1-59307-135-3 /$9.95

BLADE OF THE IMMORTAL
Hiroaki Samura
Volume 1: Blood of a Thousand
192-page B&W / 1-56971-239-5 / $14.95

Volume 2:Cry of the Worm
176-page B&W / 1-56971-300-6 / $14.95

Volume 3: Dreamsong
208-page B&W / 1-56971-357-X / $14.95

Volume 4: On Silent Wings
176-page B&W / 1-56971-412-6 / $14.95

Volume 5: On Silent Wings II
184-page B&W / -56971-444-4 / $14.95

Volume 6: Dark Shadows
192-page B&W / 1-56971-469-X / $14.95

Volume 7: Heart of Darkness
192-page B&W / 1-56971-531-9 / $16.95

Volume 8: The Gathering
208-page B&W / 1-56971-546-7 / $15.95

Volume 9: The Gathering II
216-page B&W / 1-56971-560-2 / $15.95

Volume 10: Secrets
232-page B&W / 1-56971-741-9 / $14.95

Volume 11: Beasts
192-page B&W / 1-56971-746-X / $16.95

Volume 12: Autumn Frost
232-page B&W / 1-56971-991-8 / $16.95

Volume 13: Mirror of the Soul
256-page B&W / 1-59307-218-X / $17.95

GUNSMITH CATS
Kenichi Sonoda
Volume 1: Bonnie and Clyde
176-page B&W / 1-56971-215-8 / $13.95

Volume 2: Misfire
184-page B&W / 1-56971-253-0 / $14.95

Volume 3: The Return of Gray
248-page B&W / 1-56971-299-9 / $17.95

Volume 4: Goldie vs. Misty
192-page B&W / 1-56971-371-5 / $15.95

Volume 5: Bad Trip
170-page B&W / 1-56971-442-8 / $13.95

Volume 6: Bean Bandit
224-page B&W / 1-56971-453-3 / $16.95

Volume 7: Kidnapped
232-page B&W / 1-56971-529-7 / $16.95

Volume 8: Mr. V
224-page B&W / 1-56971-550-5 / $18.95

Volume 9: Misty's Run
176-page B&W / 1-56971-684-6 / $14.95

LONE WOLF AND CUB
Kazuo Koike and Goseki Kojima
Volume 1: The Assassin's Road
296-page B&W / 1-56971-502-5 / $9.95

Volume 2: The Gateless Barrier
296-page B&W / 1-56971-503-3 / $9.95

Volume 3: The Flute of the Fallen Tiger
304-page B&W / 1-56971-504-1 / $9.95

Volume 4: The Bell Warden
304-page B&W / 1-56971-505-X / $9.95

Volume 5: Black Wind
288-page B&W / 1-56971-506-8 / $9.95

Volume 6: Lanterns for the Dead
288-page B&W / 1-56971-507-6 / $9.95

Volume 7: Cloud Dragon, Wind Tiger
320-page B&W / 1-56971-508-4 / $9.95

Volume 8: Chains of Death
304-page B&W / 1-56971-509-2 / $9.95

Volume 9: Echo of the Assassin
288-page B&W / 1-56971-510-6 / $9.95

Volume 10: Hostage Child
320-page B&W / 1-56971-511-4 / $9.95

Volume 11: Talisman of Hades
320-page B&W / 1-56971-512-2 / $9.95

Volume 12: Shattered Stones
304-page B&W / 1-56971-513-0 / $9.95

Volume 13: The Moon in the East,
The Sun in the West
320-page B&W / 1-56971-585-8 / $9.95

Volume 14: The Day of the Demons
320-page B&W / 1-56971-586-6 / $9.95

Volume 15: Brothers of the Grass
352-page B&W / 1-56971-587-4 / $9.95

Volume 16: The Gateway into Winter
320-page B&W / 1-56971-588-2 / $9.95

Volume 17: Will of the Fang
320-page B&W / 1-56971-589-0 / $9.95

Volume 18: Twilight of the Kurokuwa
320-page B&W / 1-56971-590-4 / $9.95

Volume 19: The Moon in Our Hearts
320-page B&W / 1-56971-591-2 / $9.95

Volume 20: A Taste of Poison
320-page B&W / 1-56971-592-0 / $9.95

Volume 21: Fragrance of Death
320-page B&W / 1-56971-593-9 / $9.95

Volume 22: Heaven and Earth
288-page B&W / 1-56971-594-7 / $9.95

Volume 23: Tears of Ice
320-page B&W / 1-56971-595-5 / $9.95

Volume 24: In These Small Hands
320-page B&W / 1-56971-596-3 / $9.95

Volume 25: Perhaps in Death
320-page B&W / 1-56971-597-1 / $9.95

Volume 26: Struggle in the Dark
312-page B&W / 1-56971-598-X / $9.95

Volume 27: Battle's Eve
300-page B&W / 1-56971-599-8 / $9.95

Volume 28: The Lotus Throne
320-page B&W / 1-56971-600-5 / $9.95